AAT Level 4

Personal Tax

For FA2018 2018/19 Study

By Tom Davies

First edition 2020

ISBN 9798 6139 5998 3

Published by KD Publishing

The contents of this course material are intended as a guide and while every effort has been made to ensure the contents are correct at the time of publication this is not a guarantee. The author accepts no liability for any loss or damage suffered by a person acting or refraining from acting as a result of this book.

Contents

Introduction

This book on Personal Tax combines the module specification with my own personal experiences to create a guide to the module, a complete and simple way to learn the course material as well as exam techniques and tips.

I never failed any of my exams, that's not to brag, merely to suggest that I have a relatively straightforward way of learning and passing exams, which this book aims to pass on to you.

Throughout my accountancy training I was always struck by the exorbitant cost of learning materials which, when paired with other exam and registration fees, made me consider that many intelligent students from poorer backgrounds might not ever have the means to become accountants.

This book is in part me 'paying something back' and hoping that in providing this low cost option everyone has the opportunity to learn and become an accountant.

I also want to talk briefly about belief. There's no reason why you can't pass this unit. It's quite material heavy but it's absolutely doable. As Henry Ford once said, "whether you think you can, or you think you can't - you're right".

The first step is knowing that you can do this. So as you go through this book keep thinking to yourself, every chapter you read you're just that little bit closer to passing.

Frequently textbooks contain a lot of waffle, so I've tried to keep that to a minimum.

Good luck!

Chapter 1 - Exam Technique

You need 70% to pass this exam. Which is quite a lot really, but don't let that phase you, you're used to it by now and when you understand the basics you can easily pick up a lot of marks.

As with the other units 80-89% gets you a merit and 90%+ gets you a distinction. For some people that matters, for others any pass will do!

It's a 2.5 hour exam across 13 tasks and that's quite a long time, so pace yourself. It's not an easy exam but equally it isn't hugely time pressured. AAT want you to be able to take the information and decide what to do with it and they appreciate that you need the time to do that.

Read the requirement in the question first, then start reading through the information provided. Don't jump straight into an answer.

In the exam you're given quite a lot of information and it can at first feel a little overwhelming, but don't be. Be methodical and it's not nearly as bad as it first seems.

The other thing about personal tax is more or less everything is tested, there's nowhere to hide! But consider this a blessing too. If there's one particular part you really struggle with, it's not going to be make or break if you mess it up.

In terms of weighting, there's 10% for principles and rules of tax, 28% for calculating total income, 23% for calculating income tax and national insurance, 27% for capital gains tax and 12% for inheritance tax.

So when I said to you if there's one bit you can't do don't worry too much, you can see why. One part of the exam I do feel gets a heavy weighting though is capital gains, so make sure if there's one area you focus on a little more that it's here.
It's also a slightly more difficult part of the exam for most students, so if you're looking to get a Merit or Distinction it's also worthwhile to put a bit more work in here.

As with everything, practice makes perfect. Having the knowledge is one thing, being able to apply it is another.

That's why it's so important that you familiarise yourself with the AAT software and layout of the question types. I cannot recommend strongly enough that after you finish this book you attempt the practice exams. The layout and type of question will be almost exactly the same in the real exam so it really is worthwhile. Sometimes AAT are particularly lazy and those that did the practice exams get lucky because the questions are so similar you almost feel you've done them before.

It's also really useful to get used to the way the computer based assessment works with the various dropdowns, dates on a calendar and drags. It's not always the most intuitive so having a good level of familiarisation pays dividends (but more about them in the Business Tax unit!)

Written Questions:

It's crucial to understand what the question is actually asking you to do, or you'll waste time answering a question AAT didn't ask. It's amazing how many people do this!

If you're asked to **Explain** then you need to describe, in detail, what the question is asking about and write about the meaning and implications of it. It's the word AAT use when they want a longer answer from you for a question worth a higher number of marks.

If you're asked to **Discuss** then instead you need to set out a narrative, talk about what you could do and the positives and negatives of doing that.

If you're asked to **Identify** then you are being asked to pick out the correct or relevant answer or point, with only a short amount of writing needed. It's the word AAT use when they don't want you to say too much and the question isn't for that many marks.

Notes Page

Chapter 2 - Ethics & Tax Principles (10% of marks)

Learning outcomes per the AAT syllabus;

1 Analyse the theories, principles and rules of the tax system

1.1 Evaluate the objectives and functions of taxation:
- Principles of tax systems
- Tax structures & bases
- Compare progressive, regressive and proportional tax criteria

1.2 Differentiate between tax *planning,* tax *avoidance* & tax *evasion*
- Know the definitions of each one
- Understand the ethical implications of them
- Know what to do to report suspect tax evasion

1.3 Roles and Responsibilities of a Tax Practitioner
- The expectation AAT has of members per the Code of Professional Ethics
- The principle of Confidentiality
- Dealing with clients and third parties

1.4 Residence and Domicile
- Know the definitions of each
- Understand how the status of each affects the tax due

As a member of AAT being ethical is vitally important. The public and regulators hold accountants to a high standard and it's important to live up to them to maintain our reputation.

As such we need to know the duties, both legal and ethical, owed to clients and the authorities (usually HMRC).

This chapter really sets the foundations for all the other chapters and taxes ahead. It should help to get you thinking about everything that is to come up.

<u>What's the purpose of tax?</u>

1. To raise money for the government to spend - Public services are funded by taxation such as the NHS.

2. To redistribute wealth from via public services - Taking money from richer people and using it to help poorer people is often a key aim.

3. To control the economy and growth - If the government wants to encourage spending and grow the economy it might cut taxes, while if the economy is already doing well it might wish to increase taxes.

4. To provide incentives or disincentives - Government often uses taxes to make people do less of something. For example taxes on smoking and alcohol are high because the government sees it as undesirable.

<u>How does it work?</u>

The government takes the Tax Base (the thing or group to be taxed) and levies a Tax on it or them. This Tax can be Progressive and increase with the Tax Base, Proportional where the rate is always the same or Regressive, where the tax rate falls as the Tax Base increases. Most taxes in the UK are progressive.

Put simply the tax base x the tax rate is the amount which will be raised.

The Tax Year in the UK runs from 6 April to 5 April the following year. The Tax Year is also referred to as the fiscal year. For example tax year Within each Tax Year the tax due is calculated.

For AAT FA2018 the Tax Year runs from 06/04/2018 to 05/04/2019.

Most taxpayers are employees and so have tax deducted at source via a system known as Pay as You Earn (PAYE). Those who are self employed or have a capital gain to declare, as well as in some specific instances when employed, will have to complete a Tax Return.

<u>What are the principles?</u>

There are 5 principles in the Tax & Ethical Framework which you'll need to know, these are Neutral, Efficient, Simple, Certain and Effective:

Neutral - This means that taxpayers would be neither encouraged or discouraged from doing what they're doing by the tax.

In reality this is not always the case as the government often uses taxation to influence behaviours and decisions people make.

Efficient - Administering the tax shouldn't be excessively expensive. Otherwise it's a waste of the tax money. An example of this was when the government stopped collecting a certain type of National Insurance on a monthly direct debit as this was expensive to run.

Simple & Certain - Taxes should be straightforward for people to understand so that they are not caught unaware or penalised.

Simple taxes also provide less ability and incentive for tax evasion to occur.

Again, in reality this is not always the case.

Effective - The tax should do what it's intended to do and it should raise the revenue expected of it for the government to collect when it expects it.

What about Residence and Domicile?

Residence relates to physically being in the UK for a tax year, while Domicile is longer term and based on links to a Country.

Domicile is a more legal concept. There are **three** types of Domicile; Origin, Dependence and Choice.

Origin - When you are born you generally take on the Domicile of your father.

Deemed - Wherever your legal guardian is Domiciled you will also be until the age of 16.

Choice - You must leave your Country (after 16) and settle in another permanently.

If a person is Resident & Domiciled in the UK in a tax year (and that's most people) then UK income is taxed and so is overseas income (although double taxation agreements apply).

If a person is Non Resident but UK Domiciled then UK income is taxed, but foreign income is not.

If a person is Resident but Non-Domiciled then UK income is taxed, but foreign income may or may not be depending on whether the Remittance Basis is used. If it is then only income which enters the UK is taxed, but a Remittance Basis Charge must be paid.

<u>What are all the taxes I need to know about?</u>

Income Tax - Taxes regular employment and net profit received by individuals.
This is a progressive tax which rises as income goes up.

Capital Gains Tax - Taxes one off disposals of assets, such as the disposal of a property.
This is also a progessive tax, but much less so.

Inheritance Tax - Taxes the transfer of wealth. There are also tax implications on lifetime gifts.
This is a proportional tax, with a set rate once a certain threshold is reached.

National Insurance - Taxes salary and net profits and is a regressive tax as it is (loosely) linked to pensions.
As such when enough tax has been paid to cover the pension the rate falls.

<u>How are Taxes Decided?</u>

Taxes are made by statute, that is to say the MPs in Parliament approve an Annual Finance Act following the budget each year.

The taxes are initially created by Civil Servants before finding their way into a budget if approved.

After being approved the Act of Parliament is judged in Court by a Tax Tribunal and becomes Case Law, ie the interpretation the courts have of the taxes in the budget that was approved.

What Responsibilities are there?

AAT Members and Accountants have a responsibility to Clients but also to HMRC. They must act in the best interests of the client but must also deal with HMRC according to the law and ethical standards.

Remember the acronym PIPCO;

Professional Competence & Due Care
Integrity
Professional Behaviour
Confidentiality
Objectivity

Specifically Confidentiality will come up a lot. We have to be very mindful of client confidentiality and disclose only with their permission unless there is a legal obligation or professional right to do so.

Accountants also should not use privileged information for personal gain.

Of note is that a Tax Return may be prepared by an Accountant, but it always remains the responsibility of the client/taxpayer.

A client should always approve a Tax Return before submission.

Tax Planning, Avoidance and Evasion Differences

Planning - Using tax law to plan and legitimately reduce the tax bill. Perfectly legal and advisable. For example, paying into a pension scheme to gain tax relief.

Avoidance - Potential abuse of law via loopholes to reduce tax bill. May be legal, but unethical. Generally difficult in the UK because of laws which mean HMRC can retrospectively reclaim lost taxes.
A bit of a grey area and a good example of where a discuss question may arise in an exam.

Evasion - Illegally reducing the tax bill. Making up expenses, failing to declare income etc.

What should HMRC be told?

We should only disclose with the permission of the client unless HMRC issue a legal notice requiring the information, in which case the law obliges confidentiality be broken.

If there are errors then the client should be strongly advised to disclose. If they refuse then the accountant should resign and report potential Money Laundering.

Quick Questions (answers on the next page)

1. Which of these taxes is not progressive?

Income Tax
Capital Gains Tax
National Insurance

2. What dates does the UK Tax Year run?

1 January - 31 December
6 April - 5 April
1 April - 31 March

3. Which of these is not one of the five Tax Principles?

Neutral
Efficient
Positive
Simple

4. What is the Domicile of Origin?

Where you were born
Where your father was born
Where your sibling was born

5. Investing in an ISA is an example of?

Tax Planning
Tax Avoidance
Tax Evasion

Answers:

1. National Insurance, which is regressive as the rate falls as income rises.
2. 6 April - 5 April
3. Positive
4. Where your father was born
5. Tax Planning

Notes page

Chapter 3 - National Insurance (5-9% of marks)

Learning outcomes per the AAT syllabus;

3 Calculate income tax and National Insurance (NI)

3.4 Calculate NI contributions for both employees and employers
- Work out which taxpayers need to pay NI
- Calculate NI due from employ*ers*
- Calculate NI due from employ*ees*

This is a relatively small part of the syllabus but it's fairly straightforward and should be considered 'easy marks'!

Types of National Insurance

There are 4 different types of National Insurance;

Class 1 - Employment
Class 2 - Annual Self Employment
Class 3 - Voluntary
Class 4 - Self Employment

This chapter will focus on Class 1 National Insurance, as that's what you'll be tested on in the exam, so for the purposes of this unit Personal Tax do disregard the others. If you're studying Business Tax then Class 2 and 4 will be studied as part of that.

There are 3 parts to Class 1 National Insurance. It's split into Primary, the cost to the employee, Secondary, the cost to the employer and Class 1A which is also payable by the employer on non-cash benefits.

Class 1 Primary - Employee

This is a cost to the employee and you'll note the rates go up and then down, this is because it was originally tied to the state pension. The rates are;

0%   £0 - £8,424
12% £8,424 - 46,350
2%   £46,350 -

This is paid on salary and any bonus. It does not include non-cash benefits such as mobile phones which is dealt with by Class 1A later on.

Certain things are not treated as earnings and these regularly pop up in the exam. For example if an employer reimburses a necessary business expenses then this payment should not be considered income.

There are certain exemptions which you'll read more about later on.

Example: An employee has a salary of £45,000 and receives a £10,000 bonus

The employee has been paid a total of £55,000.

The first £8,424 is free from Employees NI at 0%

From £8,424 up to £46,350 Employees NI of 12% is due, £46350 - £8424 = £37,926 @ 12% = £4,551.12

Above £46,350 2% is due, £55,000 - £46,350 = £8,650 @ 2% = £173

Total employees NI due = £173 + £4,551.12 = £4,724.12

Class 1 Secondary - Employer

This is the NI cost to the employer and isn't taken out of the salary of an employee. The rates and bands are different to that which the employee pays. The employer bands and rates are;

0%   £0 - £8,424
13.8% £8,424 -

But there is an employment allowance of £3,000 which should be deducted from the total NI bill.

Example: An employer pays 5 employees £20,000 each. The total employers NI bill would be;

£20,000 - £8,424 tax free band = £11,576 @ 13.8% = £1,597.49 per employee.

£1,597.49 x 5 employees = £7,987.44

Less Employment Allowance of £3,000 = £4,987.44 payable.

Employment Allowance

As you saw above, an employer can claim £3,000 as employment allowance against their total Class 1 Employer NI bill.

However some employers are classed as excluded employers and can't claim this. There are specifically 3 categories which are excluded;

1. Businesses which do household and domestic work
2. Public authorities and public services
3. Companies where the director is the only employee

Class 1A National Insurance

This is paid by the employer on the cash value of non-cash benefits.

A non-cash benefit can be a mobile phone, a computer etc. and as well as the cost of the benefit itself an employer must also pay Class 1A on top.

The calculation for this is simple. The same 13.8% is used, except there's no bands, so simply take the cash value of the benefit and work out 13.8% of it.

For example if a £1,000 phone were given to an employee the Class 1A due would be £138. It's that straightforward.

Reimbursements

We mentioned briefly above about reimbursed expenses not being counted towards income for NI purposes.

There is an important distinction to make here. Reimbursed genuine expenses as part of doing the job are not counted towards income for NI. But private expenses are.

The classic example is phone calls. If an employer were to reimburse an employee for business phone calls, that would be fine and no NI would be due. If the costs of making private phone calls were reimbursed however then NI would be due.

There are specific reimbursements allowed for mileage and this is 45p per mile for the first 10,000 miles and 25p per mile thereafter. Anything above this is taxable for NI (both employers and employees).

<u>Tax Planning</u>

There is some scope to save tax here for an employee. An employee pays NI on cash benefits, ie salary and bonus, but does not pay NI on non-cash benefits. As such instead of a pay rise an employee may wish to receive additional non-cash benefits instead.

It doesn't make any difference to the employer who pays 13.8% on cash benefits and non-cash benefits.

Quick Questions:

1. Who pays Class 1 Primary?

Employers
Employees
The Government

2. How much Class 1 Primary is due on a salary of £15,000?

£789.12
£453.45
£723.67

3. Which of these businesses would not be able to claim employment allowance?

A hairdresser
A law firm
An NHS Trust

4. If an employer gave an employee a non-cash benefit worth £500 what would the Class 1A due be?

£74
£122
£69

5. Which of the following wouldn't be an exempt reimbursement for NI purposes?

Employer paying parking for a business trip
Employer paying for stationary for an employee to use at work
Employer paying for groceries for an employee

Answers:

1. Employees
2. 15000 - 8424 = 6576 x 12% = £789.12
3. NHS Trust falling under the public exemption
4. 500 x 13.8% = £69
5. The groceries

Notes Page

Chapter 4 - Employment (8-10% of marks)

Learning outcomes per the AAT syllabus;

2 Calculate a UK Taxpayer's Total Income

2.1 Calculate income from employment
- Employment income from salary, commissions and bonuses
- Taxable benefits in kind
- Exempt benefits
- Allowable and exempt/disallowable expenses

3 Calculate Income Tax & National Insurance payable by a UK Taxpayer

3.2 Apply relief for pension payments and charitable donations
- For private pension schemes
- For occupational pension schemes
- For charitable donations

3.5 Tax Planning techniques to minimise tax liabilities
- Maximise exemptions and reliefs
- Tax efficiency in benefits in kind
- Making investment income tax efficient
- Other changes to reduce tax

This is a really popular part of the syllabus for AAT to examine. It's the bread and butter for accountants working in tax, this is very much day to day activity. Really make sure you can calculate and explain benefits in particular.

This chapter will also take into account what you've read in the previous chapter on National Insurance.

It looks at the different types of employment payment, rules for being paid and helps you understand the difference between employment and self employment and how to decide whether someone is employed or self employed.

We'll also take a look at employment benefits to determine which are taxable.

Employment Income

First we look at the different types of employment income. There are 3; Salary, Bonuses and Benefits.

They're all self explanatory and it should be obvious in a question which of these is being referred to.

Employers have to deduct income tax at source from employees in the UK. This is known as Pay as You Earn (PAYE). Tax is due and deducted on salary, bonuses and benefits.

Employees as such receive their income net of income tax.

Because of this most employees do not need to complete a Tax Return.

In the exam you'll be given the gross pay figures and the tax deducted.

Basis of assessment

This is how we work out which tax year income is to be taxed in. There are a set of standard rules which apply to most people, but a few extra ones specifically for directors.

Normal payment of salary, bonus and benefits are treated as received at the earlier of when a payment is physically made and when a person becomes entitled to a payment.

This is particularly important for bonuses. An employee may be entitled to a bonus in one tax year, but receive it in the following tax year after the 5th April cut off. In this instance it's when the payment entitlement arose, so even though the bonus wasn't paid until after April it's treated as if it was paid the previous year for the tax calculations.

For Directors there are extra rules, as they're in a position to potentially manipulate their own employment for tax benefit.

Fore Directors any payment is treated as being received on whichever of these comes earliest:

1. Date the payment was received
2. Date the Director was entitled to the payment (these first 2 rules are the samel)
3. Date the amount is credited in the company's records
4. Date of the company's accounting period
5. Date the amount is determined

Employed or Self Employed?

There is no one answer to this question. Each example must be decided on a case by case basis and we must consider the following;

1. Level of control over the person doing the work. The more control there is, the more likely the person is to be an employee.

2. If the person has to accept the work. If they have to do the work they're likely to be an employee.

3. If the person or company has to provide further work. If they provide a continuous amount of work to a person that person is more likely to be an employee.

4. If the person provides their own equipment. If they do they're much more likely to be self employed.

5. If the person hires their own staff. This would imply autonomy and as such self employment.

6. If the person takes on the risk of the job/contract. The higher the risk and reward the more likely it is to be self employment.

7. If the person can work when they choose and determine their own hours. This makes them much more likely to be self employed.

8. Whether the contract is *for* services or *of* service. The wording of the contract will be an important determinant. If for services then it's self employment, ie a specific task for a specific time period. If it's of service then it's employment.

In your exam it's likely to be very obvious which of employed or self employed it's meant to be.

<u>Taxable Benefits</u>

Benefits are perks provided by employers for employees that are not exclusively job related.

If the employee has paid for some of the benefit themselves remember to deduct that part.

As usual, AAT like to put benefits in mid year so you may need to time apportion the months.

There are many types of benefit so please do take time to familiarise yourself with each.

1. Car Benefit & Fuel Benefit

If an employer provides a company car there will be car benefit. This may or may not be provided with fuel, but if fuel is provided then there's an additional fuel benefit to consider.

Car benefit is based on the list price of the car plus the cost of any added options less any contribution made by the employee. So a new car worth £25,000 which had £1,000 in extras and which the employee paid £3,000 towards would have a cost for benefit purposes of £23,000. Ignore any discounts as benefit is based on list price.

The % used for benefit then varies depending on what CO2 emissions the car in question puts out and whether it's petrol or diesel - you'll need to refer to the rates table below which will be tabbed in the exam.

You'll see that the % benefit rises as the CO2 emissions go up, with a premium on 4% on diesel cars which don't meet the RDE2 standard.

You'll also see there's a line at the top for 0g/km which is for electric cars, which get the most beneficial rate.

The Car Benefit Table:

CO₂ emissions in grams per kilometre	Appropriate Percentage (Electric & Petrol Vehicles)		Adjustment to Appropriate Percentage (Diesel Vehicles)
	2018-19	2019-20	2018-19 to 2019-20
0 (Electric)	13%	16%	n/a
1-50	13%	16%	
51-75	16%	19%	
76-94	19%	22%	
95-99	20%	23%	
100-104	21%	24%	
105-109	22%	25%	
110-114	23%	26%	
115-119	24%	27%	Add 4% up to a maximum of 37% for diesel cars that are not certified to the Real Driving Emissions 2 (RDE2) standard.
120-124	25%	28%	
125-129	26%	29%	
130-134	27%	30%	
135-139	28%	31%	
140-144	29%	32%	
145-149	30%	33%	
150-154	31%	34%	
155-159	32%	35%	Add 0% for cars which are certified to the RDE2 standard.
160-164	33%	36%	
165-169	34%	37%	
170-174	35%	37%	
175-179	36%	37%	
180-184	37%	37%	
185-189	37%	37%	
190-194	37%	37%	
195-199	37%	37%	
200-204	37%	37%	
205-209	37%	37%	
210-214	37%	37%	
215 or more	37%	37%	

I definitely wouldn't waste time learning the numbers in the table off by heart (unless you're very keen!) it's easier to simply look them up.

Look out for the need to time apportion if the car is not available for the whole year.

For example, if an employee was given a new petrol car with 132 g/km CO2 emissions costing £20,000 and they were given it on 1 October then the calculation would be:

27% x £20,000 = £5,400 x 6/12 months = £2,700.

Note that 'pool' cars also exist. These are provided for work with only incidental private use, which is not normally kept overnight by an employee and which is used by multiple employees.

Fuel Benefit is more simple. If fuel is provided by the employer for private mileage then there will be a benefit.

The % used is the same as the one used on the car benefit.

But instead of the list price plus options less deposit figure used to calculate car benefit, the percentage is based on a set figure, the same for all cars regardless of value, which for 2018/19 is £23,400.

As such continuing on from the car above, the calculation would be:

27% (same as car benefit) x £23,400 (same for all cars) = £6,318 x 6/12 months = £3,159

The question would then normally require you to add the car and fuel benefit together to create a total figure.

Note that if an employee pays for their own fuel there would be no fuel benefit charged.

2. Vans

The car and fuel benefit above applies only to cars. Vans are treated completely differently.

There is a flat £3,350 charge for van benefit for a van with private use, no CO_2 % to be calculated. Note that unlike for cars, a van journey from home to work does not count as private use.

There's also a £633 charge for van fuel benefit if fuel is made available for private use.

3. Other Assets

If an asset owned by an employer is used by an employee for private use then they will be charged the higher of;

1. 20% of the value of the asset when it was first made available
2. The rent paid by the employer (if any)

4. Gifts of Assets

Occasionally an asset will be gifted from an employer to an employee. The benefit which arises depends on whether the employee already had use of the asset gifted to them.

If the asset was already used by the employee the benefit of the gift is the higher of:

1. The market value of the asset when it was gifted
2. The value of the asset when it was first used by the employee less any benefit already charged

For example if the employer gifted an asset that was originally worth £1,000 and the employee had been using it previously and the employee had already paid 20% of the value (as in Other Assets above) equivalent to £200, and the asset was now worth £750 then the figure to be used would be £1000 - £200 = £800. As this is higher than the MV of the asset when gifted.

If the asset gifted is a new asset and the employee has previously had no private use of it, then the employee is charged the cost of that asset.

If the employee makes any payment towards the asset then deduct this from the value.

5. Beneficial Loans

This isn't particularly common in the real world but in your exam it come up quite commonly as it's a little bit more complex.

A beneficial loan is money leant from the employer to the employee with an interest rate lower than the market rate the employee would otherwise have had to pay.

The benefit is the difference between the interest that should have been charged had it been at market rate and the interest that actually was charged by the employer.

However if the loan amounts total £10,000 or less we just ignore it/them. If there are multiple loans you'll need to combine them.

Often there will be a repayment made in the year, so we'll need to time apportion and use what's called the Average Method.

Here's an example:

A loan of £30,000 was made to an employee. The market rate on this loan would have been 5%, but instead the employee agreed to pay £500 a year in interest. The employee also paid back £15,000 halfway through the year.
The Average Method requires we average the amounts that were due in the year:

£30,000 was due for 6 months, therefore £30,000 x 6/12 = £15,000
£15,000 was due for the other 6 months, therefore £15,000 x 6/12 = £7,500

The average amount owed for the year was £15,000 + £7,500 = £22,500.

The market interest rate would have been 5% x £22,500 = £1,125

But the employee had already paid some interest so we deduct this from the total.
£1,125 - £500 paid = £ 625 taxable benefit.

6. Accommodation

There are two types of accommodation provision, either job related or non job related.

If the accommodation is job related then there is no taxable benefit.

In order to be job related it has to meet certain criteria:

1. It must be provided for security reasons (senior politician)
Or
2. It's necessary to do the job (lighthouse keeper)
Or
3. It's an industry standard to provide accommodation (pub landlord/lady)

If the accommodation is not job related then there is a taxable benefit, calculated in two parts.

Part 1. Basic Charge

This is the higher of the Annual Value and the Rent paid by the employer. Both of these figures will be given to you in the question, you just need to pick the higher of the two

Part 2. If the employer owns the building and the value is over £75,000 there's an Accommodation Charge.

This is the Cost of the building minus £75,000 x the official interest rate.

Add the two to make a total but deduct any amount paid by the employee paid towards the accommodation.

Note: If the accommodation was acquired more than 6 years before provision to the employee the accommodation charge is based on the market value at the start of the tax year the employee started living there.

Example: An employer gives an employee accommodation near their job. It is not job related. The annual value of the property is £3,000 and the employer doesn't pay any rent because it owns the building. The building is worth £100,000 and was purchased last year. The official interest rate is 2%.

Answer: As it's not job related there will be a benefit. Because the employer owns the building there is no rent to compare the annual value to, therefore the annual value has to be higher so is the figure to use.

The building is worth in excess of £75,000 so we need to calculate an Accommodation Charge: £100,000 building value - £75,000 = £25,000 x the rate of interest 2% = £500.

£3,000 annual value + £500 accomodation charge = £3,500 benefit.

7. Accommodation Living Expenses

As well as the accommodation itself an employer may also meet the living expenses of the employees which reside there.

This can be anything from heating and running costs to repairs and furniture.

The benefit depends on whether the accommodation is job related.

If the accommodation is job related then the benefit is the lower of the cost of the expenses and 10% of the employees net earnings.

If the accommodation is not job related then the benefit is the cost of the expenses.

Example:

Accommodation which is job related is provided to an employee. The employer also meets living expenses at the property equal to £3,000 for the year.
The employee earns £29,000 and receives £2,000 of other taxable benefits. What is the benefit?

The benefit is the lower of the cost of the expenses, £3,000, and 10% of the employees net earnings = £29,000 + £2,000 = £31,000 x 10% = £3,100. Therefore the £3,000 cost to the employer is used.

8. Vouchers

The employee is taxed on the cost of the vouchers to the employer.

If the voucher can be returned or exchanged for money then the exchange cash value is used rather than the face value of the voucher.

Sometimes vouchers are exempt (see next page).

9. Exemptions

There are a lot of exempt benefits and it's worth having an awareness of these, though most of them are in the references and tables given in the exam.

1. Job related accommodation as previously explained.

2. Free or discounted food made available to all staff. Watch out for this because in the exam sometimes free food is made available to managers only, and this would be a benefit of the cost to the company less any payments made by the managers.

3. Removal expenses up to £8,000 when the employee needs to move for the job. The excess of anything over this is a benefit.

4. Car parking spaces near work.

5. Taxi fares after 9pm if the employee worked late. This cannot be regular however.

6. Pool cars, as already discussed.

7. Workplace childcare nursery or creche, but only if employer operated.

8. Externally provided childcare up to £55 per week for a basic rate taxpayer, £28 for a higher rate taxpayer and £22 for an additional rate taxpayer. Any excess is a benefit.

9. Employer contributions to an approved pension scheme.

10. Recreation or sports facilities provided by the employer. If they aren't provided by the employer but the employer pays for them then this is a taxable benefit.

11. Counselling services for employees made redundant, but only if they've been employed full time for at least two years.

12. Staff events up to £150 per head. If the event costs more per head than this the entire amount is taxable, not just the excess. This one comes up quite a lot.

13. Incidental expenses such as phone calls and laundry up to £5 per night if working away in the UK or £10 per night if working abroad.

14. Mobile phones are exempt if a single phone is provided. Additional phones are a benefit.

15. Working from home allowances of £4 per week if required to work from home (ie not a choice).

16. Bus subsidies which an employer pays toward or the provision of a bus for at least 9 employees to commute.

17. Cycles and safety equipment for commuting.

18. £50 per head for non-cash gifts to employees with 20+ years of service.

19. Staff suggestion scheme awards.

20. Air miles

21. Training which is work related.

22. £500 of medical treatment to get an employee back to work.

23. £250 of gifts from a single third party (note this does not necessarily imply it's ethical)

24. Gifts made by the employer to the employee outside the work space, such as marriage or civil partnership gifts.

10. Allowable Deductions & Expenses

General Rule: Expenses must be incurred wholly, exclusively and necessarily in the job role. That is to say, the employee had to incur the expense to do their job.

Common allowable deductions which come up in the exam are:

1. Professional fees and subscriptions, for instance to the AAT.
2. Travel expenses on the job.
3. Contributions to an approved occupational pension scheme.
4. Payroll deduction scheme charitable donations.
5. £4 a week home expenses incurred when working from home (also mentioned in exempt benefits).

Expenses

The treatment of expenses depends on if they were reimbursed by their employer or not.

If they weren't reimbursed then the employee just deducts the cost of any expenses from their income. For instance if an employee with a salary of £20,000 incurred allowable expenses of £500 not reimbursed then the employment income would be £19,500.

If the employer does reimburse the expenses then this is exempt. That is to say, there is no benefit, they're not added on to income.
As such the employee will no longer need to claim for a deduction and this makes the process quite easy.
In the exam if the employer has reimbursed allowable expenses just ignore it, you don't need to make any entries.

Statutory Mileage

When an employee uses their own car on business there is a cost to them. HMRC as such created the Statutory Mileage Scheme. This allows employers to pay employees for their mileage with no benefit, up to a set amount.

That amount is;

45p per mile up to 10,000 miles
25p per mile above 10,000 miles

Any amount in excess of this is a benefit, and any amount under this can be 'topped up' by claiming the difference as an expense.

Here are two examples:

1. An employee gets paid 50p per mile and does 10,000 miles in a year.

The employee is therefore paid £0.50 x 10,000 = £5,000.
The mileage scheme allows 45p per mile = £0.45 x 10,000 = £4,500

Therefore the difference is a £500 benefit.

2. An employee gets paid 20p per mile and does 5,000 miles in a year.

The employee is paid £0.20 x 5,000 = £1,000
THe mileage scheme allows 45p per mile = £0.45 x 5,000 = £2,250

The difference is therefore a £1,250 allowable expense deduction.

Entertaining Customers

If an employee entertains customers on behalf of the employer then the netting off as seen in the mileage allowance scheme is used.

If an employee incurs £300 of entertaining costs and the employer reimburses £300 then there is no benefit and no expenses.
If the employer were to pay £200 then the £100 shortfall would be an expense.
Likewise if the employer paid £500 the excess £200 would be a taxable benefit.

Do note however that the expense has to be specific. If the employee is given what's called a 'round sum allowance' (and it will be called this in your exam) then the whole amount of this allowance is taxable.

Pensions

As mentioned previously, an employee can save tax by making pension contributions.

Maximum Tax Relief is the higher of £3,600 and the employee earnings for the year.

Excess contributions can still be made but the employee won't receive any relief.

Tax is relieved at the marginal rate of tax and as such is saved at 20% for a basic rate taxpayer, 40% for a higher rate taxpayer and 45% for an additional rate taxpayer.

The way in which employees get this tax relief depends on the type of pension:

Personal Pension Scheme: This is paid into by the employee by themselves and is not part of a workplace scheme. Contributions are made net of 20% tax (ie at 80%) and so are grossed up.
For higher and additional rate taxpayers there is further relief on the extension of the basic rate band for income tax.

Occupational Pension Scheme: As the name suggests, this is provided by the employer. Contributions are deducted from salary and as such the tax bill is reduced by the marginal rate.

Employer contributions are not taxable and there's no limit on the amount of contributions.

Charity

Employees may wish for their employer to make a donation to charity straight out of their earnings.

Just like the occupational pension scheme, the amount is deducted from salary before tax is calculated on the remaining earnings, therefore saving the employee tax at their marginal rate.

You may see this called Give as You Earn (GAYE).

Tax Planning

There's significant scope here for an employee to reduce their taxable income.

Where possible an employee should pick exempt benefits over taxable ones and where taxable benefits are chosen should pick benefits with a lower cash equivalent value.

There are a lot of deductions as we've just seen and it's easy to miss them. So making sure all the allowances and deductions are actually claimed for is important.

Where possible taking benefits over cash is preferable as this saves on NI.

As we've just seen, paying into pension schemes can be very advantageous, especially for employees paying tax at a higher rate.

Quick Questions:

1. What premium is added on top of the benefit % for diesel cars which are not RDE2 compliant?

0%
4%
7%

2. An employee is given a diesel car emitting 101 g/km of CO_2 with a list price of £15,000 which is used privately, but the employee pays for their own fuel. The car meets RDE2 standards. What is the car benefit charge?

£3,150
£3,300
£4,100

3. An employer makes a van available for an employee with private use and also provides fuel. What is the total charge?

£4,000
£3,983
£3,821

4. An employer provides a loan to an employee of £7,500 and asks for no interest. The market rate of interest would have been 3%. What taxable benefit is there?

£0
£100
£750

5. What would be the mileage allowance for an employee with 12,000 allowable miles?

£4,500
£5,000
£5,400

Answers:

1. 4%
2. £15,000 x 21% = £3,150. No diesel surcharge as RDE2 standard. No fuel benefit.
3. £3,983, the combination of van and van fuel benefit charges.
4. £0 as the loan is below £10,000 so there is no benefit.
5. 10,000 miles @ 45p = £4,500 + 2,000 miles @ 25p = £500 = £5,000

Notes Page

Chapter 5 - Property Income (8-10% of marks)

Learning outcomes per the AAT syllabus;

2 Calculate the total income for a UK Taxpayer

2.3 Calculate property income
- Profit/loss from both furnished and unfurnished properties

3 Income Tax and National Insurance payable

3.5 Tax planning to minimise tax liabilities
- Claim all relevant exemptions and reliefs
- Make investment income more tax efficient
- Other changes that minimise tax

AAT like examining topical real world areas and this is certainly one of those. There have been significant changes to rental property rules in recent years and it's important to be able to advise clients

Property Income

As the name suggests, property income is money derived from letting or renting out land and/or property.

Rental income is calculated within each tax year, running 6th April to 5th April the following year and you may be required to time apportion rents so look out for that.

From the rental income we deduct allowable expenses in the same period. Allowable property rental expenses are those which are incurred on an ongoing basis, they are not one offs such as new central heating.

Allowable rental property expenses are:

- Ground rent, rates (such as water and council tax) and insurance
- Repairs and maintenance
- Mortgage interest but more about that shortly because there's an important treatment of the interest
- Bad debts and other finance costs
- Professional fees such as legal fees and management fees

Note that only the mortgage interest counts as an expense and tax credit, not the repayment part so you may have to break it down.

Also be aware that capital expenditure is not an allowable expense for deduction against property income. Things like new boilers, furniture and kitchens are not incurred on an ongoing basis. Instead these things are used against any capital gain on the sale of the property. See capital gains chapter.

There is, however, a replacement allowance for replacing certain items. This replacement allowance is equal to the cost of the replacement plus the cost of disposing of the thing being replaced. Qualifying assets include furniture, TVs and electrical goods and white goods.

Capital Allowances

Capital allowances are available for assets used in the course of letting out the property, but this will generally be quite rare.

If it does show up in the exam, simply take the asset value and claim the allowance over the useful life or reducing balance rate given in the question.

For example if Plant & Machinery used cost £1,000 and the question told you if had a useful life of 10 years, you simply take the £1,000 and divide it by 10 years to get a Capital Allowance of £100 for the year. With the asset value carried forward then being £900.

Alternatively the question may tell you that the asset is worth £1,000 but capital allowances are claimed at a reducing balance of 18%, in which case in our example the capital allowance expense would be £180 and the asset value carried forward would be £820.

Mortgage Interest

The government decided to limit mortgage interest expenses to try and reduce the number of landlords. Rather than all of the mortgage interest being an allowable expense, for 2018/19 tax year 75% of the interest is instead given as a 20% tax credit and the remaining 25% is allowed as an expense.

How does this work? Here's an example. Rental income is £10,000 for the year and total mortgage interest is £4,000.

Rents	£10,000	
Mortgage Int.	£1,000	(this is 25% of the £4,000 total)
Profit	£9,000	
Tax @ 20%	£1,800	
less;		
20% tax credit	£600	(this is the other 75%, £3000 @ 20%)
Tax due	£1,200	

Why does this matter? Well, for a basic rate taxpayer it doesn't, their tax bill will be exactly the same. But for a higher rate taxpayer where they only receive a 20% tax credit for three quarters of the mortgage interest they are losing out, because as an expense they were getting relief at their marginal rate of 40%.

Multiple Properties

On the tax return there is one consolidated page for Land & Property. This means the rents from every property let out needs to be combined as do all the different expenses into their relevant categories.

For example if a client has two properties, property one has rents of £12,000, house insurance of £400 and management fees of £1,000 and property two has rents of £10,000, house insurance of £300, repairs of £1,500, and management fees of £1,200 then the pooled total would be;

	£
Rents	22,000
Insurance	700
Management Fees	2,200
Repairs	1,500
Profit	17,600

Time Apportioning

AAT love putting expenses that were only incurred for part of the year in questions and properties which were bought and rented part way through the year.

For example if a property was purchased on 1st October and rented at £2,000 per month, and home insurance was taken out on 1st January the following year at £50 per month you would need to time apportion to April the following year.

1 October to the start of April is 6 months, so 6 x £2,000 = £12,000 in rent to declare.

Likewise 1 January to April is 3 month, so 3 x £50 = £150 as the house insurance expense.

Keep an eye out for this.

It's also worth noting that for calculation purposes we actually ignore the fact the tax year goes to 5th April and instead pretend it's the 1st of the month, ie we only do full months in the calculations.

Losses

If the expenses and capital allowances in the year add up to more than the rents then the client will have made a loss on that property.

Unlike some other types of losses there's not so much we can do with property losses. We can't carry it back to previous years to offset against profits from previous years and we can't use the losses against other forms of income like employment.

The property losses can only stay with property and must be carried forward to the next tax year, where they can be offset against future profits.

Note that because the rental income is pooled there will be an overall profit or loss, so any losses incurred by individual properties will automatically net off if multiple properties are rented out.

Furnished Holiday Lets (FHL)

Most people let out property empty or as a home long term for tenants. But also tested will be the rules around Furnished Holiday Lets.

As the name suggests, a Furnished Holiday let is a property which is furnished and let out to holiday makers on a short term basis.

There are some specific rules which must be met for a property to be defined as a FHL;

1. The property must be in the UK or European Economic Area
2. It must be furnished
3. It must be available to be let for at least 210 days a year
4. It must be actually let out for at least 105 days a year
5. Holiday tenants can't stay for more than 31 days in a row or more than 155 days in total each year

There are tax advantages to be had as a FHL rather than a regular property let;

1. Income can be put straight into a pension scheme because of classification as business income

2. Capital Allowances are far more generous and can be claimed on the furniture rather than having to use the Renewals Allowance.

FHL income is treated separately to regular property income and there is a different tax return page for it. In the exam do not combine FHL rents and expenses with regular rental expenses and rents!

FHL losses are also restricted, they can't be offset against regular property income nor any other income like employment. They can only be carried forward for use against future FHL profit.

Tax Planning

Property income from regular rentals and FHL is classed as non-savings income and taxed at 20%, 40% or 45% depending on the marginal rate.

As such if a client has a partner and they are not working or paying a lower rate of tax it would be beneficial to have the property in their name to pay a lower rate of tax. This is very important given the mortgage interest restriction, as a higher rate taxpayer will be significantly worse off.

Assets between married people/civil partnerships can be transferred on a nil gain nil loss basis and as such pay no Capital Gains Tax.

Quick Questions:

1. Which of these isn't an allowable expense against rental property income?
House insurance
Management Fees
New Kitchen

2. If an asset worth £10,000 is used in the property business and the asset has a useful life of 20 years what would be the capital allowance claimed?

£500
£1,000
£2,000

3. If a property is rented out from 1st July 2018 how much rent needs to be declared?

9 months worth
12 months worth
3 months worth

4. If mortgage interest is £8,000 for the year, what is the 20% tax credit?

£600
£1,200
£1,000

5. If a furnished property is let out for 110 days and was available for 200 days can it be classed as a FHL?

Yes
No

Answers:

1. New Kitchen, because that's a capital expenditure
2. £10,000 / 20 = £500
3. 9 months worth, because 1 July 2018 to the following April is 9 months.
4. £8000 x 75% x 20% tax credit = £1,200
5. No, because it needs to be available for 210 days each year to qualify

Notes Page

Chapter 6 - Taxable Income (8-10% of marks)

Learning outcomes per the AAT syllabus;

2 Calculate total income

2.2 Calculate income from investments
- The Personal Savings Allowance
- Identify taxable investment income
- Identify exempt investment income

3 Calculate Income Tax and National Insurance payable

3.1 Calculate Personal Allowances
- Calculate Personal Allowances and Restrictions on them

3.2 Relief of pension payments and charitable donations
- Private pension scheme relief
- Qualifying charitable donations relief

3.5 Tax Planning to minimise tax liabilities
- Claim exemptions and reliefs
- Make investment income tax efficient
- Other changes to minimise tax

This is where it gets interesting! This is where we take all the taxes you've read about in the previous chapters and we pile them all in together to work out what the total income is that tax is going to be due on.

This is a key part of the work an accountant will do for their client, so being able to bring all the different sources of income together and make sense of it is really important.

After all, that's what the client is paying for.

Net and Taxable Income

We're going to take this in two parts. First off we're going to look at net income, which is the combination of all the types of income we've looked at.

Then we take that net income, deduct from it the personal allowance (the tax free amount) and this produces the taxable income.

In the exam you'll be presented with a table like this:

	Non-Savings Income	Savings Income	Dividends	Total
Employment	X			X
Property	X			X
Interest		X		X
Dividends			X	X
Net Income	X	X	X	X
Less;				
Personal Allowance				(X)
Taxable Income	X	X	X	X

Net Income

Here we add non-savings income (employment, self employment, pension and property income) to savings income (interest received) and dividends.

Interest received is paid gross.

The tax rates for dividends are different to other sources of income:

Basic rate taxpayers 7.5%
Higher rate taxpayers 32.5%
Additional rate taxpayers 38.1%

We also need to remember that exempt income does not go here. We do not include exempt income in the net income calculations.

Exempt Income

As well as that which has already been mentioned in previous chapters we must also consider Individual Savings Accounts (ISAs) which are tax free.

These are special savings accounts where £20,000 can be invested and dividend and interest received from this is tax free. There are now an array of cash ISAs, share ISAs and junior ISAs.

Capital growth on the amount invested is also free from Capital Gains, which we'll explore in later chapters.

Other exempt income which may be in your exam:

1. Damages awarded because of personal injury.
2. Grants for students. Note if paid to parents it is taxable as employment income.
3. Winnings from the lottery and gambling.
4. Premium bond prizes.

Net income example:

So now let's take an example and compile the entries into the first part of the table, as you saw above, to find net income.

Tom has £30,000 of employment income from his job. He has some investments from which he has received £100 in interest and £500 in dividends. He also rents out a second property and receives income of £5,000 from this.

Net income table:

	Non-Savings Income	Savings Income	Dividends	Total
Employment	£30,000			£30,000
Property	£5,000			£5,000
Interest		£100		£100
Dividends			£500	£500
Net Income	£35,000	£100	£500	£35,600

Taxable Income

Taxable Income taxes the Net Income table one step further and deducts the various tax allowances from the income.

However before we do this we need to explore the various allowances that you'll need to decide or calculate.

The most important of which is the Personal Allowance. This is £11,850 for 2018/19. It applies to all of the income in your net asset table, but is used against non-savings income first, then savings income and finally dividend income should any personal allowance remain.

This is because non-savings and savings income is taxed at a higher rate.

But not everyone gets a full personal allowance. There is a restriction on the personal allowance for high earners which you must be aware of.

For incomes over £100,000 the personal allowance is reduced.

The amount it is reduced by is £1 for every £2 over £100,000. Remember this!

For example if earnings are £110,000 the personal allowance is reduced by £5,000.

This means that when earnings reach £123,700 the personal allowance is eliminated altogether.

If a taxpayer makes Gift Aid or Personal Pension payments the these are deducted from net income before the restriction on the personal allowance is calculated.

Each taxpayer also receives an Interest Allowance. This is £1,000 for a basic rate taxpayer, £500 for a higher rate taxpayer and £0 for an additional rate taxpayer.

As such most people don't pay any tax on interest received. Any excess above this amount is taxed at the same rates as income tax.

Each taxpayer also receives a £2,000 dividend allowance, regardless of what marginal rate they pay.

Example 2

Tom has employment income of £50,000, no property income, savings income of £500 and dividends of £1,000.

	Non-Savings Income	Savings Income	Dividends	Total
Employment	£50,000			£50,000
Interest		£500		£500
Dividends			£1,000	£1,000
Net Income	£50,000	£500	£1,000	£51,500
Less;				
Personal Allowance (£11,850)				(£11,850)
Savings Allowance		(£500)		(500)
Dividend Allowance			(£1,000)	(£1,000)
Taxable Income	£38,150	£0	£0	£38,150

Tax Planning

Married couples and civil partners can reduce their tax liability by making use of all available allowances, splitting income where practical to do so to do this.

Additionally making use of the lower marginal rates can save a lot of tax.

This is especially true for dividends where a basic rate taxpayer only pays 7.5% on dividends while a higher rate taxpayer pays 32.5%.

Investing in tax free products will also help to reduce the tax liability. From the exempt income section ISAs are particularly popular and useful for taxpayers to save tax. So making use of the ISA allowance is an easy way to pay less tax.

High earning taxpayers can preserve their Personal Allowance by paying into pension schemes and by making qualifying charitable donations.

Quick Questions:

1. What is the personal allowance if a taxpayer has £105,000 of net income?

£11,850
£9,350
£8,000

2. What is the taxable non-savings income if Tom is a higher rate taxpayer and received £600 in interest?

£100
£600
£0

3. What are the taxable dividends if Tom received £2,000 of dividends and he is an additional rate taxpayer?

£0
£1,000
£2,000

4. What is Tom's net income if he has employment of £20,000, property income of £7,500 and receives interest of £500?

£20,000
£28,000
£30,000

5. What is Tom's taxable income if he has employment of £20,000, property income of £7,500 and receives interest of £500?

£14,500
£15,650
£28,000

Answers:

1. £5,000 / 2 = £2,500. £11,850 - £2,500 = £9,350
2. £600 - £500 allowance for a higher rate taxpayer = £100
3. £0 as this is covered entirely by the Dividend Allowance
4. £28,000. Remember, net income is before allowances
5. £27,500 - £11,850 pa = £15,650. The interest is covered by the savings allowance.

Notes Page

Chapter 7 - Income Tax (10-13% of marks)

Learning outcomes per the AAT syllabus;

3 Calculate Income Tax and National Insurance Payable

3.2 Relief for pension payments and charitable donations
- Relief for occupational pension schemes
- Relief for private pension schemes
- Relief for charitable donations

3.3 Income Tax Computation
- Calculate income tax from all income sources
- Using the correct tax rates and tax bands
- Remembering to take into account income tax deducted at source

3.5 Tax Planning to minimise tax liabilities
- Relevant exemptions and reliefs
- Making investment income more tax efficient
- Other changes to reduce tax liabilities

This is the next part in bringing everything you've read in the previous chapters together. So you understand the different taxes, you know how to work out taxable income, now we're going to look at the tax due on that taxable income.

As per the last chapter, this is an important part of the job of an accountant in letting their client know how much tax they need to pay and reducing that tax bill where legally possible.

Income Tax

This may look a bit overwhelming at first but don't worry, it's very methodical.

Let's start with a review of all the different income types and the tax rates applicable to them at the different levels of income:

	Non-Savings	Savings	Dividends
Basic Rate £0-34,500	20%	20%	7.5%
Higher Rate £34,501-150,000	40%	40%	32.5%
Additional Rate £150,000+	45%	45%	38.1%

From this we determine the Net Income, before deducting any applicable allowances to leave us with the Taxable Amount.

Also a reminder of the allowances;

Personal Allowance £11,850 for 2018/19, but reducing by £1 for ever £2 over £100,000.

Savings Allowance £1,000 for Basic Rate, £500 for Higher Rate and £0 for Additional Rate Taxpayers.

Dividend Allowance: £2,000 for all taxpayers.

Finally a reminder of Gift Aid & Personal Pension Schemes:

These are paid net (80%)

A Basic Rate Taxpayer gets relief at source. A Higher Rate Taxpayer grosses up the payment (100/80) and extends their basic and higher rate bands to obtain further relief.

1. Non-Savings Income

Non-Savings Income (Employment, Pension & Property) is taxed first. The lower rate bands are used up first before moving on to the higher rate bands.

Example: Tom earns £165,000 in employment income for the year and £20,000 in property income.

Total the two together to get £185,000 of net non-savings income.

Because the income is so high all of the Personal Allowance is eliminated.

£34,500 of the income is taxed at basic rate 20% = £6,900
£150,000 - £34,500 = £115,500 of higher rate is taxed at 40% = £46,200
Then the £35,000 over £150,000 is taxed at 45% = £15,750.

The total income tax bill is therefore £68,850.

2. Savings Income

After we've taxed non-savings income we then tax the savings income.

It's likely at this point the personal allowance has been used up by the non-savings income, but if it hasn't we can use the remaining amount against savings income.

Remember also the Savings Allowance.

Example:

Tom has an employment which pays him £8,000 a year. Tom also receives £5,000 in interest. What is the tax on savings?

The personal allowance is £11,850 - £8,000 of it is used by the employment = £3,850 left.

We then deduct this from the interest received. £5,000 - £3,850 = £1,150.

Tom is a basic rate taxpayer and therefore receives a £1,000 savings allowance.

£1,150 - £1,000 = £150 taxable at 20% = £30.

3. Dividend Income

Finally we look at the dividend income received. At this point it's likely the non-savings and savings income has used up the personal allowance and at least some of the basic rate band. This is the last slice of income taxable at the marginal rate.

Remember the £2,000 dividend allowance needs to be taken off and that the rates for taxing dividends are different from those used to tax savings and non-savings income.

Example:

Tom receives £30,000 net income from his employment and £5,000 in dividends. What is the tax due on the dividends?

Firstly we have to deal with the non-savings income. £30,000 - £11,850 personal allowance = £18,150 of taxable employment non-savings income.

£34,500 basic rate band - £18,150 = £16,350 basic rate band remaining. This is enough to cover the dividends received.

Dividends £5,000 - £2,000 allowance = £3,000 @ 7.5% = 225.

Extending the tax bands

As we've mentioned, payments to personal pension schemes or to UK registered charities ('qualifying donations') attract tax relief. But how exactly does this work?

It works because the money spent by the taxpayer is essentially not taxable. So the the taxpayer saves the tax that would have been due on the income that was taxable but no longer is because of what the taxpayer has chosen to do with it.

For administration purposes the charity or pension payments made are deemed net of tax, ie at 80% and then the charity or pension scheme claims back the 20% from HMRC.

The taxpayer has gotten relief at 20% because they only paid 80% in the first place.

Thus basic rate relief is obtained automatically.

But for higher rate and additional rate taxpayers it's a little more complex.

A higher rate taxpayer is due 40% relief, so they have another 20% to claim. Likewise an additional rate taxpayer is due 45% relief, so they have another 25% to claim.

How is this done? By extending the basic rate and higher rate bands.

Remember to gross up the amounts by 100/80!

Note that this is for personal pensions - occupational pensions have tax relief at source.

Example 1: Tom earns £55,000 and hasn't made any pension or gift aid contributions;

£50,000 -£11,850 = £43,150 taxable

£0-£34,500 @20% = £6,900
£43,150 - £34,500 = £8,650 @40% = £3,460

Total tax £10,360

Example 2: Tom earns £55,000 and makes £3,000 in private pension payments.

£55,000 - £11,850 = £43,150 taxable.

Basic Rate Band = £34,500 + £3,000 x 100/80 = £38,250

£0-£38,250 @20% = £7,650
£43,150 - £38,250 = £4,900 @40% = £1,960

Total tax £9,610

You'll note the saving on example 1 is £10,360 - £9,610 = £750. This is the other 20% which has been saved in tax:

Pension payment £3,000
Grossed up 100/80 to £3,750
£750 therefore saved at source
£750 saved by extending the band
£1,500 saved total = 40% saved in total.

Tax Planning

We've seen in this chapter how important the allowances are and that we can essentially manipulate them to some extent to keep the marginal tax rate down.

It's been a standard tax planning device for many years to make pension payments, especially for a higher rate taxpayer, to make some big tax savings whilst also preparing adequately for retirement.

Expanding the bands also has the added bonus of protecting some of the other allowances such as the Savings Allowance which may otherwise have been reduced.

Quick Questions:

1. What is the savings allowance for a higher rate taxpayer?

£0
£500
£1,000

2. What is the dividend allowance for an additional rate taxpayer?

£0
£1,000
£2,000

3. What is the income tax due on £15,000 of non-savings income?

£0
£630
£3,000

4. What is the tax due on £10,000 of dividends if the basic rate has already been used up?

£750
£3,250
£2,600

5. How much is the basic rate band extended with £2,500 in Gift Aid?

£500
£625
£750

Answers:

1. £500
2. £2,000
3. £15,000 - £11,850 pa = £3,150 @ 20% = £630
4. £10,000 - £2,000 dividend allowance = £8,000 @ 32.5% = £2,600
5. £2500 / 10/8 = £3,125 - £2,500 = £625

Notes Page

Chapter 8 - Inheritance Tax - IHT (around 12% of marks)

Learning outcomes per the AAT syllabus;

1 Theories and Principles of Tax

1.4 Residence and Domicile
- The effect this has on Inheritance Tax

5 The Basics of Inheritance Tax

5.1 Chargeable Lifetime Transfers (CLTs) and Exempt Transfers
- Chargeable Lifetime Transfers
- Exempt Transfers
- Potentially exempt transfers
- Reliefs and Allowances
- Trusts

5.2 Inheritance Tax Calculations
- Tax payable on death
- Tax payable on lifetime transfers
- Payment of IHT

This may be quite different to what you're used to. Many people have at least some understanding of income taxes as we all pay them in our day to day lives. But Inheritance is a less understood area.

For this reason it's important accountants can advise clients so they can make arrangements accordingly.

This is quite a long chapter and it reflects the fact Inheritance Tax is a bit more complicated than income taxes, especially given it's only worth about 12% of the marks.

In terms of prioritising, Inheritance Tax is a relatively difficult area worth relatively few marks and while I wouldn't advise you completely ignore it because you shouldn't, this should be the last area you really get to grips with if you're struggling or under time pressure.

Introduction

Many people think of Inheritance Tax as a tax on death, but there's actually a lot more to it than that.

It's a 3 step process with different stages which have to be completed in order.

These stages are:

1. Lifetime Tax paid on Lifetime Transfers
2. Death Tax paid on Lifetime Transfers (in the 7 years before death)
3. Death Tax paid on the death estate (assets owned at death)

There are also residence and domicile considerations. A UK domiciled taxpayer is charged IHT on all of their assets regardless of where they are.

A non-domiciled taxpayer is charged IHT on their UK assets.

Lifetime Tax on Lifetime Transfers

This is when a taxpayer gifts assets during their lifetime which are subject to inheritance tax.

The gift must at first be valued. This is calculated using the 'diminution in value' concept.

This literally means 'what's the fall in value on the rest of the asset(s) that wasn't gifted?'

For a lot of gifts, it's just the value of whatever it is, say a house or a cash gift.

But for some gifts such as pieces of land or share portfolios the value used is the fall in the value of the donor estate, which may be greater than the face value of the assets.

The amount to use is always the loss to the donor, rather than the gain of the donee person receiving the gift.

For example:

Todd receives a gift of property from his uncle. The property is worth £250,000 and the fall in the value of the uncle's estate is also £250,000. In this case the diminution in value is the £250,000 fall in value of the estate, which happens to be the same as the value of the property.

Todd also receives 500 shares from his uncle worth £3 each. However the uncle's 3,000 shares which were worth £5 each before the gift, as the uncle held control of the company, are only worth £3 each after the gift as control of the company is lost.

As such the value of the gift to Todd is 500 x £3 = £1,500 but this is irrelevant.

The fall in value of the uncle's estate is:

Before 3,000 x £5 = £15,000
After 2,500 x £3 = £7,500

Fall in value £7,500. As such the diminution in value is £7,500 and this is the gift value.

Further to this there are special rules for listed shares. Quoted/listed shares are valued at the <u>lower</u> of:

1. The 'quarter up' value, which is the lower of the quoted price plus ¼ of the highest quoted price less the lowest quoted price

2. The average of the highest and lowest marked bargains.

Example:

Shares in Banana plc are gifted from Fred to Jimmy. On the date they were gifted the shares are quoted at 90-100p. The highest marked bargain was 88p and the lowest was 100p.

The value per share is the lower of:

1. Quarter up = 90 + ¼ x (100 - 90) = 92.5p

2. Average = 100 + 88 / 2 = 94p

Therefore the value per share used is 92.5p

<u>Exemptions</u>

As always there are lots of exemptions to consider.

Some are available only on lifetime gifts, while others are also exceptions for death gifts too.

There are far more exemptions during life, so it's preferable to gift assets during lifetime to avoid death taxes.

Exemptions during lifetime and death:

1. Transfers between married partners and civil partners
2. Transfers to political parties

Exemptions during lifetime only:

1. Small gifts exemption - Gifts of £250 or less per year to a donee in a tax year. There's no limit on the number of donees. Any amount above this per person is chargeable.

2. Annual Exemption - £3,000 each year can be transferred exempt from IHT. It's done in date order, so a gift made to one niece in January of £3,000 is exempt but another gift of £3,000 to a nephew in July would then not be.

Any unused annual exemption can be carried forward for 1 year, after which it is wasted.

3. Normal expenditure - IHT is a tax on transfers of capital, not a tax on income. So a transfer is exempt if it's made as part of the normal spending of a donor, taken out of income and it leaves the donor with sufficient income to maintain their regular standard of living.

4. Gifts on Marriage or Civil Partnership

    a) £5,000 from a parent is exempt
    b) £2,500 from a 'remoter ancestor' such as grandparents, aunts/uncles
    c) £1,000 from anyone else

Potentially Exempt Transfer (PET) or Chargeable Lifetime Transfer (CLT)?

So now we have determined the value of any gifts and any exemptions. Now we must consider if the gift is actually taxable or not.

A potentially exempt transfer (PET) is a gift to a person. It is <u>not</u> taxable during lifetime but will be part of the death estate if the donor dies within 7 years. They do use up the annual exemption though.

A chargeable lifetime transfer (CLT) is a gift to a trust. It <u>is</u> taxable during the lifetime and tax must be paid immediately. There is a second subsequent tax charge when the donor dies.

CLTs should be made before PETs in a tax year to make better use of the annual exemption as the exempt amount will be wasted on PETs if the donor lives more than 7 years from the date of the gift.

The lifetime tax on CLTs still takes into account the £325,000 nil rate band. Any accumulated CLTs in the last 7 years up to this are charged at 0% and any over this are charged at 20%.

Calculating the lifetime tax on CLTs depends on who is paying the tax.

If the **donee** (person receiving) is paying the tax:

1. Calculate the value of the CLT. It may be given in the exam or you may have to work it out using the principles earlier in the chapter. Remember to deduct any exemptions

2. Review the previous 7 years to work out if any other CLTs have been made and if so how much of the nil rate band (NRB) has been used.

3. Do the calculation. Any NRB left is at 0%, anything over the NRB remaining is at 20%.

Example: Steve makes a gift of £200,000 to a trust. He had already made a gift to a trust of £200,000 three years ago and has used all exemptions this year already.

£325,000 - £200,000 = £125,000 NRB left.
£200,000 - £125,000 = £75,000 @ 20% = £15,000 lifetime tax

If the **donor** pays the tax:

Instead of getting the trustees/donees to pay the tax on a CLT the donor may wish to pay the tax themselves to protect the gift amount.

For instance if a donor gave £100,000 to a trust and the trustees/donees paid the 20% tax there would only be £80,000 left in the trust.

However the tax treatment for the donor is less favourable. For the donor the gift is grossed up.

As such if the donor makes a CLT and pays the tax on a £100,000 gift the tax due is £100,000 x 20/80 = £25,000.

It's easier to simply remember that donors pay the tax at 25%.

To calculate the tax:

1. Calculate the value of the gift. This may be given to you or you may have to work it out using the principles earlier.

2. Review the previous 7 years to check if other CLTs have been made. If they have some or all of the NRB may have already been used.

3. Calculate the tax. This is the gross amount x 20/80 (25%) on the CLT over the NRB.

4. Work out the gross transfer, this is established by adding the net transfer and the tax together.

Example: Stan makes a gift of £356,000 to a trust and he wishes to pay the lifetime tax that is due. He already made a CLT 5 years ago of £200,000

First off we deduct the Annual Exemptions from this year and last year = £6,000.

£356,000 - £6,000 = £350,000

NRB Remaining = £325,000 - £200,000 = £125,000 @ 0%

£200,000 CLT - £125,000 = £75,000 x 20/80 = £18,750

Gross transfer = £18,750 + £200,000 = £218,750

Death Tax on Lifetime Transfers in the 7 years before death

So now we've considered the lifetime tax we need to consider the death tax.

IHT is charged on both CLTs and PETs made in the 7 years before death.

Gifts made over 7 years before death are exempt.

We also need to consider Taper Relief. This is given if the donor survives more than 3 years but less than 7 to make the gift exempt.

For tax planning it's therefore crucial that wealth be given away as soon as possible. Death tax is always paid by the recipient of the gift.

As with lifetime taxes there is a process to follow to calculate death tax:

1. From the date of death review the previous 7 years and locate all lifetime transfers. Whether a PET or a CLT they are now all chargeable.

2. Starting with the earliest gift made in the prior 7 years:

a) Establish the chargeable amount; value less exemptions grossed up if necessary for CLTs where the donor paid

b) Deduct from the NRB at death (£325,000) gifts in the prior 7 years. Important note that PETs over 7 years do not reduce the NRB but CLTs over 7 years ago do.

c) Deduct any remaining NRB from the gifts under consideration. The IHT rate at death is 40%.

d) Taper the tax if the gift was made more than 3 but less than 7 years ago.

Taper Relief:

Years before death	% Reduction
3-4	20
4-5	40%
5-6	60%
6-7	80%

e) Deduct any lifetime tax paid. Note that this cannot generate a tax rebate.

3. Repeat step 2 for each gift made in the previous 7 years.

Death Tax paid on assets at death

The final part of this 3 stage process is to calculate the tax due on the assets owned at death, the death estate.

1. Calculate the value of the death estate

2. Apply any exemptions. Spouses/civil partners and political parties are always exempt. Remember the other exemptions were for lifetime gifts only

3. Identify all of the transfers made in the 7 years prior to death, PETs and CLTs. Deduct the gross value of these from the NRB.

4. Any NRB left should be deducted from the death estate. The remaining death estate is taxed at 40%.

Example:

	£	£
Death Estate		200,000
NRB	325,000	
Less CLTs/PETs:		
CLT 1y ago	(100,000)	
PET 2y ago	(50,000)	
NRB left	175,000	
Taxable at 0%		(175,000)
Taxable at 40%		25,000
IHT Payable		10,000

Spouses and civil partners

A spouse or civil partner can transfer any unused NRB on death to their significant other. A claim must be made for this.

For instance if Sarah died and had £150,000 of NRB remaining then this can be added to her husband John's £325,000 giving him £475,000 to use on his death.

Tax Planning

As discussed in the chapter, PETs become exempt after 7 years has passed, so it's very beneficial to make lifetime gifts to individuals from a younger age.

Make use of exemptions each year as they arise.

Giving assets to a trust creates a tax liability which may have otherwise been avoided.

It's increasingly popular to skip a generation. Grandparents give assets to their grandchildren and as such avoid IHT on the middle generation.

Quick Questions:

1. If Joe gifts Claire some land worth £10,000 and Joe's estate value falls from £250,000 to £225,000 what is the value of the gift?

£0
£10,000
£25,000

2. Which of these is <u>not</u> an exempt transfer?

A gift of cash to a political party
A gift of property to a spouse
A gift of land to a niece

3. A potentially exempt transfer (PET) is a gift to a:

Trust
Person

4. What is the lifetime tax on a £100,000 CLT if the NRB has already been used up, exemptions have already been used and the tax is paid by the donor?

£20,000
£25,000
£0

5. How many years after making a PET does a donor have to live for it to be free of IHT on death?

0 years
5 years
7 years

Answers:

1. £25,000
2. Gift of land to a niece
3. Person
4. £100,000 x 20/80 = £25,000
5. 7 years

Notes Page

Chapter 9 - Capital Gains Tax - CGT (around 27% of marks)

Learning outcomes per the AAT syllabus;

1 Theories and Principles of Tax

1.4 Residence and Domicile
- Definitions of each
- Effect of each on the Capital Gains Tax due

4 Capital Gains and Losses

4.1 Chargeable and exempt transactions
- Chargeable and exempt assets
- Chargeable and exempt people
- Connected persons

4.2 Taxable Gains and Allowable Losses
- Calculate chargeable (taxable) gains and losses on 'normal' disposals
- Part disposals
- Chattels and wasting chattels
- Determine Principal Private Residence (PPR) relief

4.3 Gains and Losses on the Disposal of Shares
- Matching rules
- Bonus Issues
- Rights Issues

4.4 Calculating Capital Gains Tax (CGT)
- Exemptions
- Treatment of losses
- Rates of CGT
- Paying CGT

Income Taxes you're expected to know pretty well. Inheritance Tax is where a lot of people struggle. Capital Gains is what you've got to know well enough in order to pass the exam.

It makes up arguably a disproportionate amount of the marks in the exam, but that's what AAT have decided. It's a large part of the exam with almost a third of the marks available for Capital Gains.

This is a long chapter but it's well worth investing your time here. There are quite a few parts which make up Capital Gains, such as the different types of disposal and subsequent gain or loss; from property, to shares and 'normal' disposals of assets.

Each type of disposal has different workings, reliefs and even tax rates.

Chargeable Gains

For a disposable to be taxable there must be a chargeable disposal (sales, gifts or loss of assets or the part of assets) of a chargeable asset (ie not an exempt asset) by a chargeable person (any individual).

A chargeable disposal is the sale, gifting or loss of an asset or part of an asset. There are some exemptions however, transfers on death as they're treated under Inheritance Tax rules and gifts to charities.

There are also exempt assets:

1. Motor vehicles suitable for private use (generally there would be no gain anyway)
2. UK government bonds/stocks/securities
3. Qualifying corporate bonds such as loan stock
4. Wasting chattels such as race horses
5. Premium bonds
6. Investments in ISAs

Calculating gains and losses

Firstly we have to take the disposal proceeds. This is generally whatever the asset has sold for but it's always deemed to take place at market value if the asset was a gift, given to a connected person, deliberately sold under value.

This does not include 'bad bargains' though. This is when an asset is unknowingly sold at less than the real value. For instance you hear of people paying a tenner for a £1m artwork that had been lost for decades down at the car boot sale.

If a chargeable asset is lost/destroyed insurance money may be paid out. In this case this is treated as a chargeable disposal and the insurance money is the disposal proceeds.

Secondly we must look at costs. The following costs are deducted from the disposal consideration:

1. Incidental Costs of Disposal: The costs of selling the asset such as advertising costs.

2. Allowable Costs: The original purchase price + costs of purchasing the asset such as legal fees.

3. Enhancement Expenditure: Capital expenditure which enhances the value of the asset such as a new kitchen in a rental property.

We deduct these costs from the disposal proceeds to get the gain.

If there are multiple disposals they are added together to create a net gain or loss for the year.

However before the gain becomes a taxable gain we must deduct from it the capital gains annual exempt amount, which is £11,700 for 2018/19. Note that this is not the personal allowance and is completely separate from it.

Example: Tom disposes of a £15,000 painting. The painting had cost him £1500 at a charity shop and other allowable expenses which had been incurred were £500. His other income is a £20,000 employment. What is the capital gains tax due?

First we must determine the gain:

	£
Proceeds	15,000
Less;	
Acquisition	1,500
Other costs	500
Gain	13,000
Exempt Amount	11,700
Taxable Gain	1,300

Capital gains is charged at 10% for non-residential property for a basic rate taxpayer and 20% for a higher rate taxpayer. Tom clearly has significant basic rate band left;

Employment £20,000 - £11,850 personal allowance = £8,150

£34,500 - £8,150 = £26,350 of basic rate allowance left.

Therefore the entire taxable gain of £1,300 is at 10% = £130.

Capital Losses

Capital Losses are first offset against any gains in the year, as the capital gains return is a combination of all gains and losses in the year.

If losses in the year are greater than gains there will be no capital gain and the losses can be carried forward to the next tax year.

The losses in the following tax year should only be used to the extent that they reduce the gain down to the exempt amount.

For example if there were losses brought forward of £2,000 from the previous year and there were a gain of £12,700 this year then only £1,000 of the losses would be used to bring the gain down to the £11,700 exempt amount, with the £1000 left carried forward to next year.

Extending the bands

A reminder that any Gift Aid or Personal Pension Payments which extend the basic and higher rate bands also applies for capital gains.

Self Assessment for CGT

Any Capital Gains Tax is due on 31st January the year following the end of the tax year. There are no payments on account and the entire sum is due in one payment.

Special CGT Rules

Part disposals: Sometimes part of an asset is disposed of, such as a part of a field. It's obvious enough to work out what the asset sold for given the disposal proceeds, but how do we know how much a bit of something cost?

As such there's a particular formula which you must learn. This one's really important.

Original Cost of Asset x $\dfrac{\text{Value of the part of the asset disposed of}}{\text{Value of the part of the asset disposed of + Market value of the remainder}}$

For example if the original cost of a field was £100,000 and part of it was sold for £75,000, with the remaining part valued at £50,000.

£100,000 x $\dfrac{£50,000}{£50,000 + £75,000}$ = £40,000 would be the cost of the land sold.

Chattels

Chattels: These are tangible moveable assets.
Wasting Chattels: A chattel with a remaining useful life less than 50 years.

Wasting chattels are exempt from CGT so there are no gains or losses to be calculated. They include things like machines and animals.

Low value chattels that aren't wasting are treated a little oddly:

Cost	Proceeds	Treatment
Under £6,000	Under £6,000	Exempt
Under £6,000	Over £6,000	Restrict to max of £6,000 or 5/3 of proceeds
Over £6,000	Under £6,000	Gross proceeds deemed to be £6,000
Over £6,000	Over £6,000	Calculate gain as normal

Transfers to connected persons

If a disposal by an individual is made to a connected person then the disposal is treated as having taken place at market value.

If there's a loss then this is restricted and can only be used against gains made against the same connected person.

A connected person is:

1. The spouse/civil partner of a taxpayer
2. Their children and grandchildren as well as their spouses/civil partners
3. Parents and grandparents and their spouses/civil partners
4. Siblings and their spouses

Note that despite the market value of an asset being used for spouses/civil partners no actual gain arises as transfers are treated as being nil gain nil loss.

Residence

Taxpayers with a domicile in the UK pay tax on all their gains regardless of where the assets are located.

Non-domiciled but UK resident taxpayers pay CGT on UK gains but only on remitted foreign gains.

Non-resident taxpayers pay no CGT on assets except for UK property.

Tax Planning

Make use of the Annual Exempt Amount. If it's already been used in this tax year delay gains to the next tax year to make use of it in the following tax year.

Making gains at the start of a tax year gives an extended time period to pay the CGT.

There's a nil gain nil loss transfer between spouses/civil partners and this means allowances can be made use of to the greatest extent.

This is especially important if a spouse/civil partner pays a lower rate of tax or has unused capital losses which could be used to offset against a transferred gain.

Principal Private Residence Relief

A person does not pay any capital gains tax on their main residence (with gardens up to ½ hectare).

If a person only has one property then it is the principal private residence by default.

If they have multiple properties then they must pick one as the principal private residence, with the rest being liable for capital gains tax on disposal.

If a property was part occupied then the gain is time apportioned, with the period of occupation being tax free. It's a simple calculation;

Gain   x   Period of occupation
                Period of ownership

It gets a little more complicated for temporary occupation though. There are periods of what's called 'deemed occupation' where the property may not actually be occupied but it can be treated as so.

Deemed Occupation:

The final 18 months of ownership are always deemed occupation and capital gains tax free provided the property was at any point the principal private residence.

If the owner was abroad because of their employment then this entire period is deemed occupation.

If the owner was working away but still in the UK then any period up to 4 years can be deemed occupation too, the time away over 4 years is then taxable.
A generous period of 3 years away is also deemed occupation for any other reason.

What if the property has other uses?

If the part of the main home is being used for anything other than as a residence then that portion of the home not used as a home is not covered under PPR.

For instance if a room in the main home is used as an office then this would make a portion of the home a chargeable gain on disposal.

This is done on a percentage basis depending on the number of rooms or floor space. For example if one bedroom was used for business purposes and the home had 6 main rooms then ⅙ of the property gain would be taxable.

Also of note is that people who are married or in a civil partnership only get one PPR between them. When single, each person would get their own PPR so for tax planning purposes marriage/civil partnership may not be advisable. Though it's likely this isn't the main consideration that would be given!

Another vital piece of tax planning is to make sure a client gets the deemed occupation periods. A taxpayer should return to the property after a period away to make sure they get the exemption and should sell within 18 months to take full advantage of the final 18 months deemed occupation.

Share Disposals

Share Disposals are often worth 10 marks in the exam, it's key that you can do this because it's very methodical and and you can easily pick most of these marks up.

There are rules when shares are sold, with two parts to this. First is the matching rules, where shares which are sold from a pool are matched to a particular part of that pool in order to work of the cost.

The second is to look at bonus and rights issues of shares. With these we look at the pool treatment and see how they affect the cost of the shares.

Matching Rules

This is all about working out which shares from a pool are deemed as being sold. Say you have 3,000 shares and you bought them in 1,000 batches at 3 different dates and at 3 different costs. How would you know what the base cost would be if you decided to sell 1,500 of these shares at a later date? This is where the matching rules come in.

Shares sold should be matched with purchases of the shares in this order;

1. Purchases of shares on the same day as disposal
2. Purchases of shares in the 30 days after the disposal, on a first in first out basis
3. Shares from the share pool

The share pool has all the shares ever purchased up to the day before the disposal of shares. It gets bigger when shares are acquired and gets smaller when they're sold.

Working out the value of the share pool isn't too complicated, there need to be two columns, one showing the number of shares, another showing the cost of those shares.

Each time shares are disposed of or acquired a new total share number and total cost for the share pool needs to be calculated.

Then on disposal if the pool needs to be used (remember, it's last in the matching rules, with same day purchases/acquisitions coming first, the following 30 days coming second and then the share pool last) the average cost of the pool is what needs to be used.

This is all a bit conceptual so it's best demonstrated with an example:

Tom bought the following shares in ABC Ltd;

	Number of Shares	Cost £
1st Jan 2010	1,000	10,000
30th June 2016	2,000	25,000
1st October 2018	500	10,000
30th October 2018	500	12,500

On 1st October 2018 Tom sold 3,500 shares for £50,000.

Tom needs to use the matching rules to understand the cost of the shares he sold.

1. Same day: 500 shares at a cost of £10,000
2. Next 30 days: 500 shares at a cost of £12,500
3. Shares from the share pool - remember this is made up of all purchases up to the day before the disposal:

Share pool	No of Shares	Cost £
1 Jan 2010	1,000	10,000
30th Jun 2018	2,000	25,000
Total	3,000	35,000

We need 2,000 shares from the pool to get to the 3,000 total therefore £35,000 / 3000 x 2000 = £23,333

Add up the cost of each = £10,000 + £12,500 + £23,333 = £45,833

Gain = proceeds - cost = £50,000 - £45,833 = £4,167.

Bonus Issues & Rights Issues

The second part to share disposals is Bonus Issues and Rights Issues, which just builds on what you've already read about the share pool.

Sometimes shares aren't purchased, they're simply given as a bonus for already owning shares. This is called a Bonus Issue and the bonus is given in proportion to the existing shareholding.

For example if there's a 1 for 3 bonus issue and you already own 3,000 shares then you would get 1,000 free shares to take the total to 4,000. As Bonus Shares don't cost anything, they only affect the number of shares in the pool, but not the cost.

For a Rights Issue however there is a cost. A shareholder is given the right to buy shares in proportion to their current ownership. These are usually at a discount (or else why would anyone buy them) and so because there's a cost they affect not only the number of shares in the pool but the cost of the pool too.

Again, this is best demonstrated with an example;

Tom buys 10,000 shares for £10,000 on 1 Jan 2015. On 1 Jan 2016 there's a 1 for 5 Bonus Issue. Finally on 31 December 2018 there's a 1 for 3 Rights Issue at £0.75 per share which Tom takes up.

The share pool would look as follows:

Share Pool	No Shares	Cost £
1 Jan 2015 Purchase	10,000	10,000
1 Jan 2016 Bonus	2,000	-
Sub Total	12,000	10,000
31 Dec 2018 Rights Issue	4,000	3,000
Total	16,000	13,000

The Bonus is 1 for every 5 shares, which is 2,000 bonus shares for free.

The Rights Issue is 1 for every 3 of the now 12,000 shares, which is 4,000 new shares. Each new share cost a discounted £0.75 which is a cost of £3,000.

Tax Planning

Each person gets their own Capital Gains Allowance separate to their Personal Allowance for regular income, as previously mentioned. Therefore it makes sense to make disposals each year up to this allowance to make full use of it.

This is particularly relevant to share disposals as they can be easily part disposed of, where other more tangible assets can't be.

As such a shareholder or accountant can easily calculate gains before the shares are disposed of, and can manipulate the number of shares to be sold to ensure the gain does not exceed the tax free amount.

As ever, because each person has their own allowance it makes sense to split the disposals where possible. As people who are married or in a civil partnership can transfer assets to each other with no tax implications, it makes sense to utilise both allowances fully.

Quick Questions:

1. The final how many months are deemed occupation as long as the property has at some point been occupied?

1 year
18 months
6 months
3 years

2. Which of these matching rules comes first?

Same day acquisitions
Share Pool
Next 30 day acquisitions

3. If Derek sells a vase to Samantha for £500 when he knew the actual value was £1,000 what is the disposal consideration?

£500
£1,000
£1,500

4. Which of these is not a wasting chattel?

A car
A prize donkey
A painting

5. If Tim sells a chattel costing £4,000 for £5,000 what is the treatment?

Exempt
£1000 gain
£0

Answers:

1. 18 months
2. Same day acquisitions
3. £1,000
4. The painting
5. Exempt as proceeds and cost under £6,000

Notes Page

Notes page

Notes page

Printed in Great Britain
by Amazon